YOU CAN BE A WOMAN™ PALEONTOLOGIST

Diane L. Gabriel
and
Judith Love Cohen

Illustrations:
David A. Katz

Cascade
Pass, Inc.

www.cascadepass.com

Editing: Janice J. Martin

Copyright © 1993 and 1999 by Cascade Pass, Inc.
Published by Cascade Pass, Inc., Suite C-105, 4223 Glencoe Ave.
Marina Del Rey CA 90292-8801
Printed in Hong Kong by South China Printing Co. (1988) Ltd.
All rights reserved.
Revised Edition 1999
You Can Be a Woman Paleontologist was written by Diane Gabriel and Judith
Love Cohen, designed and illustrated by David Katz, and edited by Janice Martin.

This book is one of a series that emphasizes the value of science and mathematical studies by depicting real women whose careers provide inspirational role models.

Other books in the series include:
You Can Be A Woman Engineer
You Can Be A Woman Oceanographer
You Can Be A Woman Marine Biologist
You Can Be A Woman Cardiologist
You Can Be A Woman Botanist

You Can Be A Woman Architect
You Can Be A Woman Astronomer
You Can Be A Woman Zoologist
You Can Be A Woman Egyptologist

Library of Congress Cataloging-in-Publication Data
Gabriel, Diane L., 1946-
    You can be a woman paleontologist / Diane L. Gabriel and Judith Love
Cohen ; illustrations, David A. Katz; editing, Janice J. Martin. -- 1st ed .
        p. cm.
ISBN 1-880599-43-0 (hbk.)
ISBN 1-880599-12-0 (pbk.)
    1. Paleontologists--Vocational guidance--Juvenile literature. [1.
Paleontologists. 2. Occupations.]   I. Cohen, Judith Love, 1933-   . II. Katz,
David A. (David Arthur), 1949-   ill.
QE714.7.G33   1994   93-21349
560'.23--dc20   CIP

Dedication

This book is dedicated to Diane's grandmother, Laura Correll Rome, who held Diane's hand as they explored museums of all kinds. Gram Rome started Diane on the journey through time that would bring her to the Mesozoic Era, that wondrous time, long ago, when dinosaurs ruled the world.

This book is also dedicated to Judith's daughter Rachel, who demonstrated very clearly the enormous power that images of dinosaurs have on the imagination of our children.

It is hot! The "Digging Dinosaurs Expedition" is taking a break. The volunteer participants are very eager this morning, but since they are new to this type of work, Diane Gabriel, their expedition leader, reminds them to slow down, rest, and take a drink of water.

The site is in Montana's Makoshika State Park. "Makoshika" is a Sioux word for "badlands" and only refers to the land "being unsuitable for farming." These badlands are beautiful, with multicolored wind- and rain-carved rocks filling the landscape. The sun casts changing shadows across this arid environment.

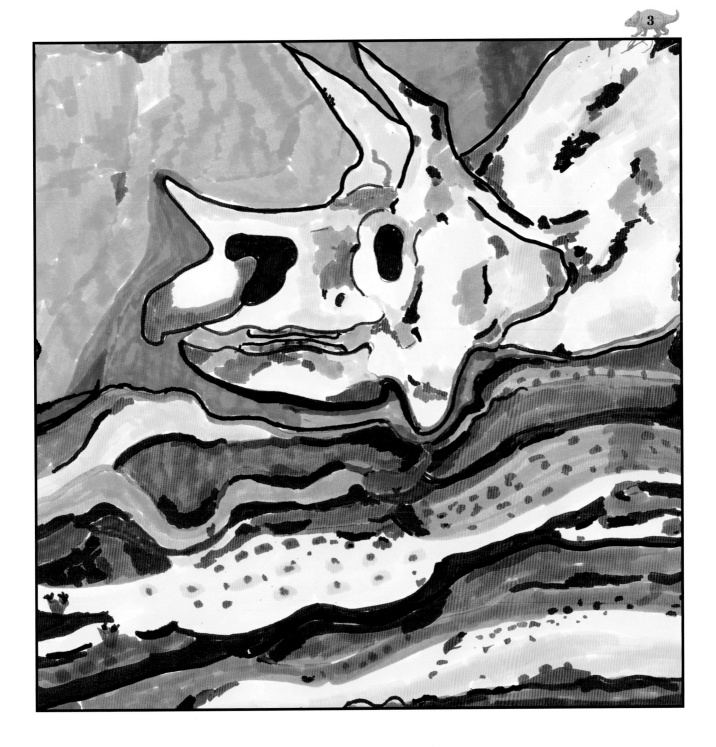

The participants might have possibly expected snowcapped mountains and icy running streams. Instead, Makoshika is a lot like the Arizona desert.

But they are here, and they are eager to make the discovery, eager to enter the world of the distant past and see where the dinosaurs walked.

Diane reminds them how to search: spread out, walk slowly and carefully, look at the ground ahead, pay attention to anything unusual in shape, color and texture. Ms. Gabriel is a paleontologist, a professional bone hunter, and she knows what kind of rocks are likely to contain fossils. She knows that this rock is the right kind, and fossils have been found before in this area. However, the technology is not precise. They may find nothing.

The participants walk up the side of the ridge, 48 eyes carefully examining every foot of exposed rock.

A young man stops and raises his hand. "There's a pointy thing over here." Diane stops the group and makes her way across the hill. "Is it a bone?" she asks. He shrugs his shoulders.

She reaches the spot and looks down at something that looks like a huge horn. Her heart beats faster. She knows that they have found a Triceratops skull!

Why is Diane Gabriel doing this? Why is she here in Montana? Let her tell us her story, the story of a dinosaur digger. . .

The most vivid memories of my childhood have water in them: tidal pools, swimming holes, the Atlantic ocean. My father taught me to catch fish and eels and showed me how to search for shells and find clams in the sand.

My indoor memories involve books. I remember being a member of the "bookworm club" in the second grade. I especially enjoyed mysteries because, like the detectives, I tried to figure stuff out.

To me, reading was an escape. I could go to other countries by reading travel books, to other times by reading history books, and I could even be other people as I read their biographies.

I also liked ancient history. The books about Egyptian pharaohs were especially fascinating to me. My grandmother took me to a museum where I actually walked through an Egyptian tomb.

I was a very good student, and my parents were pleased whenever I made the honor roll. I had always assumed I would go to college. I was in high school when my father shocked me by saying that I needed to enter the work force after graduation. But I accepted his decision, knowing that I would be good at whatever work I found.

I married a teacher who was constantly going back to school to study more, so one day I decided to take a class too. It was at the University of Massachusetts at Amherst, and the class was "Primate Behavior." In this class we studied the behavior of monkeys and apes. I was hooked.

The next thing I knew I was taking graduate courses in primate anatomy and even doing dissections. My previous experience in anatomy was boning a chicken for dinner. . .

I discovered I was very good at anatomy. Soon I was in the honors program studying anatomy and physical anthropology, and doing observational research on a live primate colony. After three years I decided that I wasn't cut out for working with live monkeys. Fossils were a lot more interesting to me.

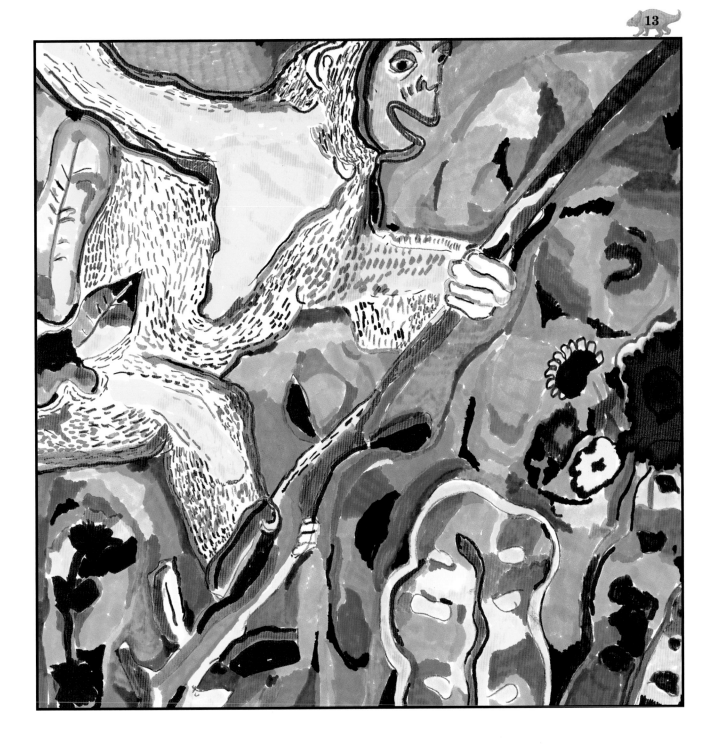

Paleontology is the study of ancient life forms. But first you need to study the anatomy of present-day animals: birds, mammals, reptiles, fish. Anatomy is fascinating. You can see what an animal was like and how it lived by studying its bones. It is necessary to know the characteristics of vertebrate (with backbone) animals.

You also need to study geology in order to understand the various layers of rock and what periods in ancient times they represent (such as Cambrian or Jurassic). The oldest rocks were obviously laid down first and started out as the deepest layers. Earth movements then caused mountains to push up and water carved out canyons to expose the oldest layers of rock. This is what you see in the Grand Canyon, where 1.5 billion years of time, from the Precambrian Era to the Paleozoic Era, is exposed.

And finally there are the bones themselves. I was especially interested in dinosaurs, so I learned about the different kinds and how their skeletons looked.

The classification of dinosaurs is difficult because dinosaurs were alive over a period of 160 million years. Also, during this time many kinds of dinosaurs evolved (changed). What we know about the dinosaurs is gathered from the study of their fossils and comparing these fossils to modern animals. During the Triassic and Jurassic Periods, from 225 to 140 million years ago, the primitive dinosaurs evolved into two major orders: bird-hipped dinosaurs which included plated dinosaurs like the Stegosaurus; and the lizard-hipped dinosaurs which included the large sauropods like the Apatosaurus.

During the Cretaceous Period, from 140 to 65 million years ago, the bird-hipped dinosaurs included the armored, horned and duckbilled dinosaurs; and the lizard-hipped dinosaurs branched out to include carnivorous dinosaurs like Tyrannosaurus rex.

Now that I knew what paleontology was, I had to learn how to do it. Fortunately, I had a chance to do research projects. Like most scientific work, this research would use the three-step scientific method: ask questions, gather information and draw conclusions.

Before scientists begin, they need to think about which questions they want answered, what kind of information to look for, and what things to study. After they have done the study, they then look at all the data and analyze it to determine what the answers might be.

One paleontologist I know, Jack Horner, asked the question "Did the dinosaurs nurture their young?" Modern reptiles are not well known for their close-knit families. On the other hand, many mammals and birds do provide extensive care for their young.

Jack Horner then asked "What kind of information should we look for? Maybe a place where dinosaurs lived with their babies? Or maybe fossils of various-sized baby animals?" That sounded like quite a tall order. But in one of the most amazing finds in paleontological history, Jack Horner discovered a site containing nests of fossilized dinosaur eggs and young dinosaur skeletons!

A lot of study followed before a conclusion could be drawn: the young dinosaurs were not just hatched from eggs and left on their own. There was good evidence that the adults were caring for these young dinosaurs. Jack called these dinosaurs Maiasaura, which means "good mother lizard."

GOOD MOTHER

When I began working as a paleontologist, my job was to collect dinosaur specimens for a new museum exhibit. The two most exciting finds made during my early volunteer dinosaur expeditions were a Torosaurus and a Stygimoloch. Our Torosaurus specimen was the largest and most complete ever found. The skull measured 9.5 feet from nose to the edge of the head frill and 8 feet across the frill at the widest point. Stygimoloch is a rare bone-headed dinosaur with fantastic horns on the back of its skull.

Now I am doing research that focuses on the bone growth of dinosaurs. The older studies of dinosaurs portrayed them as cold-blooded reptiles, like big crocodiles. Today, we see that the story is more complicated. The bones of dinosaur fossils are more like birds, and we now think of dinosaurs as "warm-blooded" in some ways.

The Cretaceous Period ended about 65 million years ago. Dinosaurs became extinct at that time. There are two major theories about what caused this extinction. One is that the dinosaurs were killed off by some catastrophe, an asteroid impact with Earth, or a volcanic eruption, or both. The other theory suggests that dinosaurs died out gradually over millions of years due to climatic changes.

My research in this area, studying dinosaur populations over the last 3 million years of their existence on earth, brought me to the badlands of Montana. There, using volunteers of the Digging Dinosaurs Expedition to find remains and collect data on kinds and numbers, we hope to census this population and find answers to what actually caused the extinction of dinosaurs.

How can you tell if you would be good at paleontology? If you can answer yes to the following questions, then you should consider becoming a paleontologist.

1. Do you have a good eye for texture, shape, forms and colors?

The studies of both geology and anatomy require the ability to recognize the differences between similar things. I have learned to look at sedimentary rocks and determine what kind of environment they represent, such as river channel or flood plain. While finding a fossil is very important, it is even more important to be able to visualize which of the many pieces of bone or tooth go together and what animals they represent.

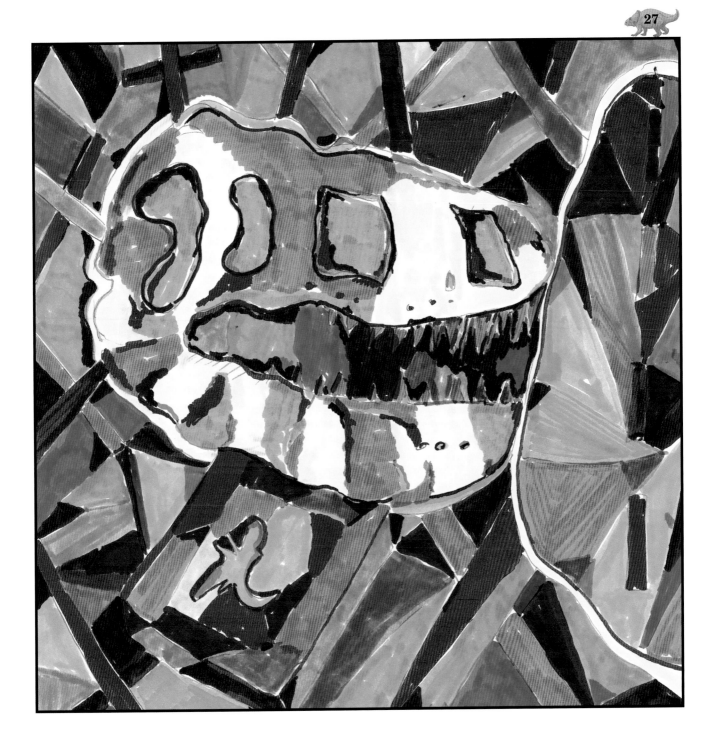

2. Do you like to go hiking in the wilderness?

While you don't have to go out in the field, that is the best part for many of us. I love to go to the badlands and see no one else for a week or two, sense the wonder of nature, and experience the elements still at work today as they have been over hundreds of millions of years.

3. Do you like to figure things out, use your imagination and make connections?

I always liked solving puzzles. As a paleontologist, I look for clues to solve puzzles, much like a detective. The length of a bone, the shape of a skull, even the structure of the bone cells might be the type of clue needed to learn something about how an animal lived so many years ago.

The best part of my career as a professional bone hunter is the summer research program. In this program we have volunteer dinosaur diggers who come to learn and help. The program has been very successful, and we collected many dinosaur specimens for museum exhibits during the early years. Now when we go out, we primarily gather dinosaur data. Only when a specimen is rare or needed for research do we collect it.

During the rest of the year, in addition to my museum responsibilities, I continue my own studies into the bone growth of dinosaurs. To do this I study the bone growth and structure of a modern animal, the ostrich, from hatchling to adult size. I will compare the ostrich bone growth stages to those of Maiasaura. I hope to determine how dinosaur bones grew, how long it took to grow from hatchling to adult, and what kind of metabolism this implies.

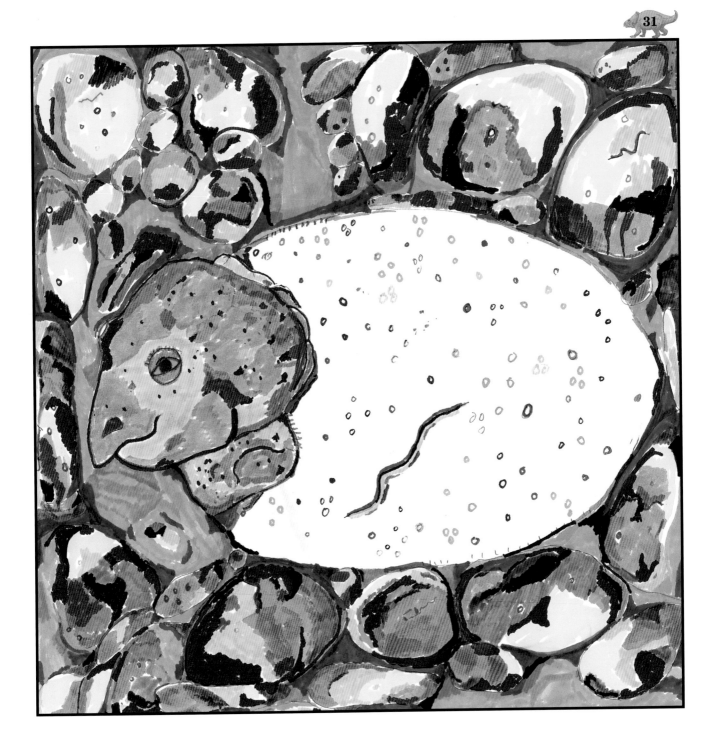

My future goals include continuing with my education. I would love to finally receive my doctoral degree. To do this I will need to complete my research on bone histology (the study of bone at the cellular level).

I also want to continue my research on the dinosaur extinction project and learn more about dinosaurs and their environment. In this way, I can bring the past to life for dinosaur enthusiasts of all ages. Many people find it hard to understand how we can learn anything from animals that are long dead. But we can, especially since new avenues of research are constantly opening to us.

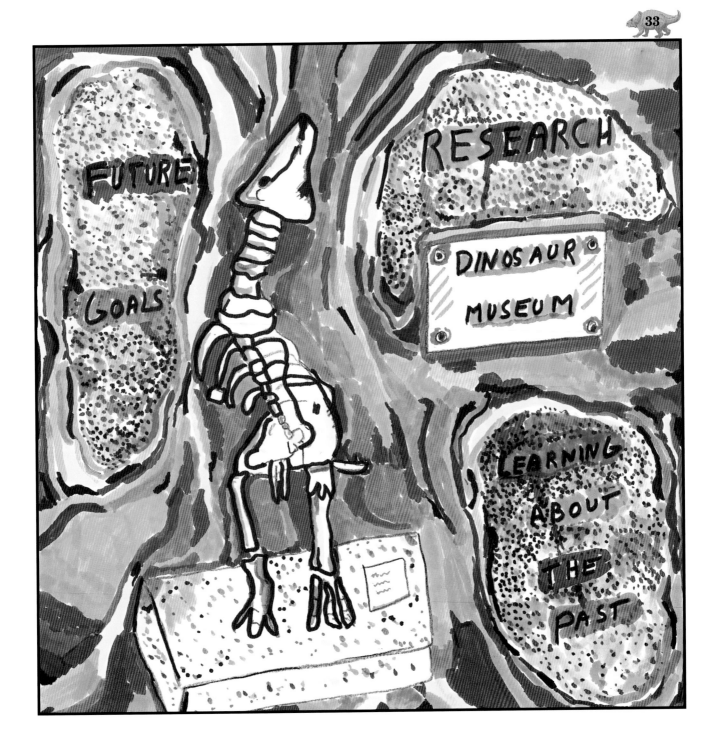

In order to be a paleontologist, all you need is a serious dedication to understanding the biology, behavior and environment of living animals, and the imagination to apply that to the fabulous creatures of the past.

If you want to figure out new things; if you want to go out and see things for yourself, like dozens of fossilized dinosaur eggs in the ground; if you want to examine the cells in a small piece of bone; if you won't be upset to find that everything you thought you knew about a subject might change in a few years by the application of new research, like dinosaurs might have a high metabolism for part of their life and a slower metabolism in another phase of their life; if you are interested in how our modern animals are related to those of the distant past, then you can do it too. You can be a woman paleontologist.

YOU CAN BE A WOMAN PALEONTOLOGIST

PALEONTOLOGY LESSON PLAN 1

PURPOSE: To gain an understanding of the variety of environments that dinosaurs lived in and how we know about them.

MATERIALS: Shoe box, scissors, cardboard, paint, paste, pipe cleaners.

PROCEDURES: Have students pick an environment and geologic age and gather pictures and facts about their era. It could be a Cretaceous Period sea floor, or a Jurassic Period swamp.

Have the children select the plants, rocks and animals that will fit into their environment.

Next, have the children create pipe cleaner animals and paint the background in their shoe box.

CONCLUSIONS: What kinds of environment and period did you choose?

What kinds of dinosaurs lived in your environment?

What kind of food were they eating?

PALEONTOLOGY LESSON PLAN 2

PURPOSE: To gain a familiarity with different features of dinosaur anatomy.

MATERIALS: Pictures of dinosaurs, crayons, scissors, pencils, large sheets of paper.

PROCEDURES: Have children divide into two or more teams. Each team will select parts of the dinosaur pictures and make a composite dinosaur, e.g., the frill of a Triceratops, the tail of a Stegosaurus, the body and legs of a Tyrannosaurus rex, the head of an Apatosaurus.

Each team tries to guess which dinosaur parts are used in the other teams' composites.

CONCLUSIONS: What features do dinosaurs have that modern animals do not have? How are the dinosaur features different from one another? Are the features similar to modern animals in any way?

RESOURCES: Library books on dinosaurs and on fossils.

PALEONTOLOGY LESSON PLAN 3

PURPOSE: To understand what fossils are and how they come to be.
MATERIALS: Clay, sand, and a variety of objects from bottle caps to chicken bones.
PROCEDURES: Have the children place some of the objects in wet clay, and bury some of the objects in sand.
Leave the objects alone for a few days. Then have the children "excavate" them and catalog them. Be careful to preserve the impression of the objects in the clay.

CONCLUSIONS: What is found in the sand? Are the objects different? Is there anything besides the object in the sand?
What do we have in the clay? What can you learn from the impression or "mold" left from the object?
What other kinds of fossils can be found in clay or sand or rock?

PALEONTOLOGY LESSON PLAN 4

PURPOSE: To appreciate the size of dinosaurs.
MATERIALS: Ball of twine or yarn (100 feet long).
PROCEDURES: Have one child hold the end of the twine or yarn and other children unroll the ball of twine, moving out of the classroom, out of the building, across the yard, however long it takes.
CONCLUSIONS: How long are some dinosaurs? (Diplodocus is 100 feet, etc.) Can you imagine a creature that is as big as your length of yarn?

About the Authors:

Diane L. Gabriel is now a research assistant in paleontology at the Museum of the Rockies in Bozeman, Montana. Prior to this, she was the assistant curator of Paleontology, Geology Section, Milwaukee Public Museum in Milwaukee, Wisconsin. She received a B.A. in anthropology from the University of Massachusetts in Amherst, has done graduate work in biology and anthropology at the University of Wisconsin in Milwaukee, and is now a Ph.D. candidate at Montana State University in Bozeman. Diane has done research work on dinosaur extinction and bone growth and development in dinosaurs. Her work has been published in many journals and has been featured on the PBS video series "Dinosaurs." She is the director of the Digging Dinosaurs Expeditions for Museum of the Rockies. Ms. Gabriel is a member of the Society of Vertebrate Paleontology.

Judith Love Cohen is a Registered Professional Electrical Engineer with bachelor's and master's degrees in engineering from the University of Southern California and University of California, Los Angeles. She has written plays, screenplays, and newspaper articles in addition to her series of children's books that began with *You Can Be a Woman Engineer.*

About the Illustrator: David Arthur Katz received his training in art education and holds a master's degree from the University of South Florida. He is a credentialed teacher in the Los Angeles Unified School District. His involvement in the arts has encompassed animation, illustration, and play-, poetry- and songwriting.